Contents

Foreword by the Archbishops of Canterbury and York

**Dr Rowan Williams,
Archbishop of Canterbury**

**Dr John Sentamu,
Archbishop of York**

Modern life can be busy and pressurized. This is especially so for families, who may find it difficult to make time to spend with each other, let alone at key times of the Christian year.

This book is designed to help families celebrate Lent and Easter together — by learning about the Lent and Easter story and doing fun things together but also taking time out for prayer and stillness and to re-connect with God's creation.

The **Love Life Live Lent** actions may also be done together, and by taking part you will be joining with thousands of others making a difference and transforming their world through simple acts of kindness and generosity.

With God's help, we can change the world for good a little bit every day. Together we can build better and more generous communities. Together we can lighten our load on the planet. We show God's love when we do these things.

Enjoy living Lent and Easter and transforming your world with your family.

How to use this book

This book is designed to help you celebrate Lent and Easter as a family. It may be used alongside the **Love Life Live Lent** booklets.

Love Life Live Lent started in Birmingham in 2006. It was a campaign to encourage people to mark Lent in a different way. Rather than giving up chocolate or going on a detox, it encouraged people to use Lent to undertake one simple act of generosity each day. The actions are small and fun to do, but make a real difference in homes, families and communities.

This book contains **Love Life Live Lent** actions for both adults and children throughout Lent. It also includes Lent and Easter activities — things to think about, make and do together.

Here are some creative ways of doing Love Life Live Lent as a family:

- Kick off Lent by holding a Pancake party on Shrove Tuesday (recipe on p. 7). Why not invite friends and neighbours to join you?

- Sit down at the start of Lent and think about how you will follow **Love Life Live Lent** as a family. You might want to make a Lenten tree, on which you can 'hang' the **Love Life Live Lent** actions as you do them. See instructions on p. 12.

- There are FREE family wall-planners you can download from the web site www.livelent.net

- Adults and children might want to have their own booklets, in order to tick off the actions as they are completed. Booklets may be ordered from www.chpublishing.co.uk

- You don't have to do all of the actions. You could choose to do all the actions from one of the six categories — for example, all the 'green' actions or all the 'global' actions.

- If you can't do the actions during the week, why not try to do at least one of them at the weekend?

- We have suggested looking up stories yourself in the Bible, or in a book of Bible stories (indicated by the Bible icon ✝). You may want to watch the scenes from a DVD instead — e.g. **The Miracle Maker** (indicated by the DVD icon 💿).

- At Easter, hold a celebration and give everyone the opportunity to share stories of **Love Life Live Lent**. What was the most important thing about it? Or use the 'Walk to Emmaus' idea on p. 47.

The little picture next to each action tells you what kind of action it is:

 Something to do at home or with those who look after you

  Something to do at school or work

 Something to help the environment

 Something to help the community you live in

 Something to help people around the world (supplied by Christian Aid)

 An action to help you pray or be quiet

*There is more help listed on the inside of the back cover for actions marked with an asterisk.

Week 1 - Kids' Actions

 **Action 1** Say something nice about someone behind their back ☐

 **Action 2** Share pancakes with your family ☐

 **Action 3** Give your pocket money to a charity that works with children overseas* ☐

Action 4 Clean up your room and take anything you don't need to a charity shop (with an adult) ☐

 **Action 5** Share a smile! ☐

 Say sorry to someone **Action 6** ☐

Adult & Youth Actions

 **Action 1** Say something nice about someone behind their back ☐

 **Action 2** Invite friends and neighbours round for a pancake party ☐

 **Action 3** Skip a meal and give the money to a charity working overseas* ☐

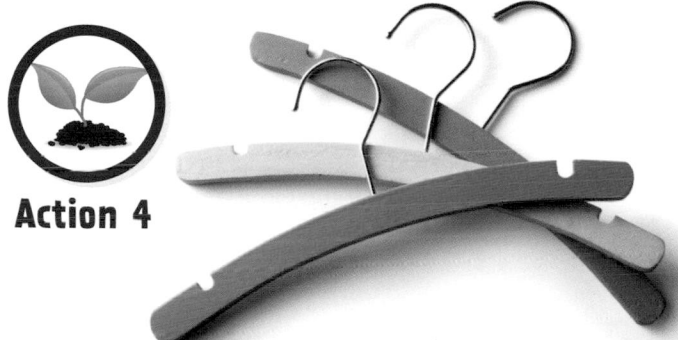 **Action 4**

Have a clear-out – take things to a charity shop, recycle or offer to others ☐
(see www.freerecycle.com and www.freecycle.com)

Give up your place in a queue to someone else ☐ **Action 5**

Action 6 Make a list of things you want to say sorry for to God– then destroy it ☐

5

Preparing for Lent
Shrove Tuesday

Lent Facts: What is Lent?

Lent is the Christian season that takes us from Ash Wednesday through to Easter. It is 40 days long (the Sundays are not counted) and is linked to the time when Jesus spent 40 days without food in the desert. It is a reminder that Jesus went through suffering to make him stronger and more trusting in God.

 You can read the story in the Bible in Matthew, chapter 4, verses 1 to 11.

 Watch **The Miracle Maker**, start of scene 2, from about 10 minutes in until 12 minutes 40.

In the early days of the Church, Lent was a time when new Christians prepared for their baptism (which was traditionally held at Easter) by being instructed in the Christian faith and through fasting (not eating food, or eating only one meal a day) and penance (being sorry for wrong things they had done and trying to put them right).

Some people today fast during Lent, or give up treats such as chocolate! They do this to help them focus on God. Some people decide to show God's love by being more kind or generous during Lent – which is what **Love Life Live Lent** is all about!

Lent Facts: Shrove Tuesday

The day before Lent. 'Shrove' comes from 'shrive', meaning to confess. People were encouraged to say sorry to God before the start of Lent. Traditionally, it was also a day to prepare for the Lenten fast by using up all the rich food in the house – particularly butter and eggs – which has led to the tradition of having pancakes on this day.

Did you know?
Shrove Tuesday around the world

- In some parts of the world, a carnival is held on Shrove Tuesday. In some places, such as Brazil, the carnival is known as 'Mardi Gras' – 'Fat Tuesday' – and is a time of fun and celebration.
- In some parts of Britain, such as Olney, Buckinghamshire, and parts of London, pancake races are held. The race in Olney originated over 500 years ago, takes place over 415 yards and is run by women who must wear skirts, aprons and head coverings. The winning time in 2008 was 69 seconds!

Shrove Tuesday Quiz (Answers on p. 48)

1. **The world's largest pancake was cooked in Rochdale in 1994. It was 15 metres in diameter and had an estimated 2 million calories. How much did it weigh?**

   A 10 tonnes **B** 3 tonnes **C** 17 tonnes

2. **Ralf Laue from Leipzig, Germany holds the world record for tossing the most pancakes in two minutes. How many did he toss?**

   A 416 **B** 986 **C** 231

3. **In some countries carnivals are held on Shrove Tuesday. What does the Latin word 'carnival' mean literally?**

   A 'Without cars'

   B 'Without crying'

   C 'Without meat'

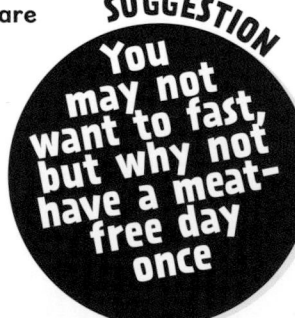
SUGGESTION
You may not want to fast, but why not have a meat-free day once

Pancake Recipe

Why not have a go at making your own pancakes and invite your family, friends and neighbours round to join in the fun? If you don't want to make your own, you can buy pancakes and add your own fun toppings.

See who can come up with the most unusual topping. What is your favourite? Who can toss the most pancakes?

Ingredients

(Makes about 12 small pancakes)

- 100 g (4 oz) flour
- 1 egg
- 250 ml (10 fl oz) milk
- 1 tablespoon of oil
  or 50 g (2 oz) butter for frying
- Pinch of salt

What to do

Note: use either metric or imperial measurements; don't mix them!

Sift the flour and salt into a basin.

Make a well in the centre of the flour, add the egg and beat until smooth. Then add the milk, a very little at a time, beating well, until you have a smooth liquid. (When you have made the batter, it is helpful to put it all into a big jug, so that you can pour a little at a time into the frying pan to make the pancakes.)

Heat a drop of the oil in a flat, thick-based frying pan. When the pan is really hot, beat your batter briefly once more and pour about 3 tablespoons of it into the pan. (Beat each time before pouring.)

Cook for just under a minute – don't forget to check underneath to see how it is cooking. Then have fun flipping or tossing the pancake!

Cook on the other side (again checking) until golden brown.

Serve with your favourite topping.

Sweet toppings
- Sugar and lemon juice
  - Maple syrup
    - Bananas
      - Chocolate spread
      - Ice cream and chocolate sauce

Suvoury toppings
Cheese, tomato, ham, beans . . .

Why not make up your own combinations?

The start of Lent
Ash Wednesday

Lent Facts: What is Ash Wednesday?

Ash Wednesday marks the start of Lent.

In biblical times, people covered their heads with ashes, or wore sackcloth (a type of rough cloth) as a sign of being sorry for the things they had done wrong.

Traditionally, on Ash Wednesday Christians had a cross-shape marked in ashes on their foreheads. This still happens at Ash Wednesday services in some churches. Sometimes the ashes are made by burning Palm Sunday palm crosses from the previous year. Being marked with a cross in ash is a sign of wanting to turn away from wrong things. It is also a reminder that every life ends. As the minister marks each person on the forehead, they say: 'Remember you are dust, and to dust you shall return.'

Have a spring clean

Lent is a time of 'clearing out' our lives: a period of 'cleansing' in preparation for Easter.

This is a good time to have a clear-out of anything you don't need any more. Unwanted items may be taken to a charity shop, or recycled. There are several web sites where you can advertise things you don't need any more: go to www.freecycle.org or www.freerecycle.org

If you have unwanted toys and children's books in good condition, could they be given to a playgroup, or to a doctor's surgery?

If you find things that belong to others, now might be a good time to return them!

Saying sorry

Ash Wednesday is a day of penitence (being sorry for wrong things and trying to put them right). One of this week's actions for children is to say sorry to someone.

Some creative 'saying sorry' activities:

- Write the word 'Sorry' in felt-tip pen on pieces of paper and put them in a bowl of water. As you watch the words dissolve, ask God to forgive you for anything you have done wrong.

- Cut out some large paper crosses. As you hold the crosses, think about the 'bad bits' of yourself that you would like to 'clear out' during Lent. (You could do this all together, or people might like to go off somewhere by themselves to do it.) After about five minutes, come back together and scrunch up the crosses.

- Write a letter to someone — or draw a picture — to say sorry. Either send the letter or picture to the person, or destroy it.

At the end of any of these activities, you might like to use this prayer:

> Dear God,
> We are sorry for the wrong things we have done.
>
> We are sorry if we have hurt others.
>
> We ask you to forgive us and help us change.
>
> Amen.

Week 2 - Kids' Actions

Action 7

Do a chore or errand for a family member ☐

Action 10

Write a letter to someone to thank them for helping you ☐

Action 8

Water some plants or a green space with washing-up water ☐

Action 11

Share a treat with someone at school ☐

Action 9

Help prepare a meal and find out where the food was grown ☐

Action 12

Think of 3 good things and say thank you to God ☐

Adult & Youth Actions

Do a chore or errand for a member of your household ☐

Action 7

Hold a fund-raising tea break ☐

Action 8

Do a garden or neighbourhood clean-up ☐

Action 9

Action 10

Leave a pound coin in a shopping trolley or somewhere else where it may be found ☐

Action 11

Buy a coffee and give it to someone on the way to work ☐

Think of 3 blessings of the day and be thankful ☐

Action 12

Caution HOT Beverage

11

Giving things up and taking things on

Lent is about giving some things up in order to focus on God. It is also about taking some things on that reflect God's character — such as doing kind and generous things for others. **Love Life Live Lent** is all about showing love to others through small, everyday actions.

Everyone is familiar with Christmas trees. You might like to make a 'Lenten tree' to have in your home throughout Lent. You may like to have it as a focus for prayer, and perhaps also use it to hang your **Love Life Live Lent** actions on, as suggested in the activity opposite.

Making a Lenten tree

To make the tree

Either draw a large, bare tree with several branches on a large sheet of paper or card, or look out for a fallen branch and put this in a pot, or somewhere else where it will stand upright.

Making the leaves

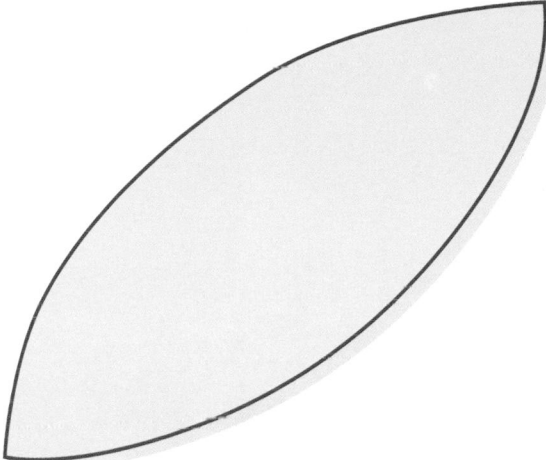

- Use the leaf template (right).

- Make copies of this (trace it, photocopy it, or download it from the web site).

- Cut out the leaf shapes.

- Write out the **Love Life Live Lent** actions on the leaves. (You might want to include all the kids' actions, or a mixture of adults' and kids' actions.)

- Put all the leaves in a box or container.

- Each day, it is someone's turn to pick out a leaf that has the day's action on it.

- When the action has been done, hang the leaf on the tree — either by sticking it onto your picture or, if you have a branch, hanging it on the tree using cotton or string.

Prayers around your Lenten tree

You might want to use your Lenten tree as a focus for family prayers. You could say a prayer after you have hung your action for the day on the tree, or after your evening meal, for example.

Prayer

Lord Jesus, thank you for this day.

Be with us as we travel through these weeks of Lent.

Help us to show your love by being kind and generous to others.

Amen.

On Easter Day, you can decorate your tree with yellow and gold ribbons, to celebrate Jesus' resurrection and completing **Love Life Live Lent** together.

Other ways of being generous

Grace Jar

Many people like to collect money during Lent and then give it away to others at the end of Lent. If you want to do this as a family, you might like to try making a grace jar.

Making a grace jar

Use an old glass jar with a screw-on top, or an empty tin with a lid (for example, a syrup or cocoa tin). Make a paper label to fit the jar, and label it: 'The Love Life Live Lent Grace Jar'. You can decorate the label too.
Some ways of gathering up the money:

- Put some money in before each meal as a 'thank you' for having enough to eat.

- Put in pocket money.

- Put in money saved by giving up treats such as chocolate or crisps.

- Raise money by doing a carwash, path sweeping, dog walking, or making things to sell at church or school, such as biscuits, cakes, bookmarks . . .

At the end of Lent, send the money to a charity — perhaps one working with children in the developing world (contact details at the back of the book).

You might like to use this prayer:

> Help us, dear God, to live with thankful and giving hearts.
>
> Help us to be kind and generous to others who are in need,
>
> This day and evermore. Amen.

Where you live

As a family, draw a map of the area you live in. Mark on it:

- The good bits — be thankful for these
- The places that need improvement — what can you do to help? Are there neighbourhood clean-up programmes you can join in with?

Life facts

Who are the 'left out' people in your community?

- In the UK 1.25 million older people say they are often or always lonely.
- At least 500 people sleep on the streets every night in England. (This is an estimate, so the real figures may be much higher.)
- It is estimated that every year in the UK 100,000 young people run away.

Is there a local project you can help by giving your time and money?

Week 3 Kids' Actions

Action 13

Don't watch TV or play on the computer – do something with your family instead ☐

Action 16

Read a story to a younger child ☐

Action 14

Make sure you say 'please' and 'thank you' all day ☐

Action 17

Save trees – use both sides of the paper ☐

Action 15

Find out about the countries where your clothes are made* ☐

Action 18

Spend five minutes by yourself quietly ☐

Adult & Youth Actions

Action 13

Action 16
Half the world lives on £1.40 a day – can you? ☐

Have a TV-free evening and do something with your household instead ☐

Action 17

Walk or cycle a route you would normally drive ☐

Action 14
Use a 'buy one get one free' and give one away ☐

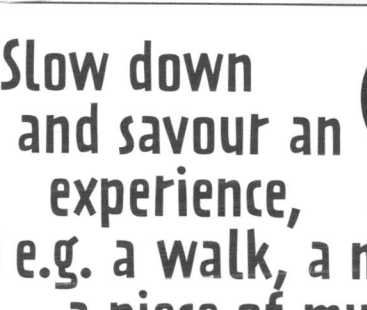

Action 15
Limit yourself to checking emails or texts only once today ☐

Slow down and savour an experience, e.g. a walk, a meal, a piece of music ☐

Action 18

17

Creative ways of praying in Lent and Easter

Lent has traditionally been a time of reflection and of prayer. Love Life Live Lent encourages generous actions — this includes being generous by spending 'quality time' with God.

Family life today can be hectic, and it can be hard to find space to pray together. Here are some creative ways of making space for God as a family:

Create a 'sacred space' in your home

You might like to create a space in your home to encourage quiet reflection and prayer. This could be:

- A corner of one room
- An understairs cupboard (it has been tried!)
- A shelf
- A corner of a shed or garage
- A space around your Lenten tree (if you are using one)
- Or make a 'prayer den', using furniture and blankets!

You might want to add objects, such as a piece of cloth, a cross, a candle, pictures of Jesus, postcards, or natural objects such as pebbles, shells or feathers.

Lent and Easter colours and objects

You might like to add different-coloured cloth and objects to your space as Lent progresses.

The colour that is used in churches during Lent is purple, so you might wish to use some purple cloth in your 'sacred space' to start off with. The colour changes to red on Palm Sunday. You might also want to add some palm branches or greenery to your space then.

On **Maundy Thursday**, remove the cloth altogether. You could add a glass of wine and a bread roll at this point, to represent the Last Supper.

On **Good Friday**, remove the glass of wine and bread roll. Add objects representing the crucifixion, such as some nails, or a branch with thorns.

On **Easter Sunday**, go to town by adding gold cloth, flowers, eggs — anything to create an atmosphere of celebration. You could also add a rolled-up bandage, to represent the grave clothes found by the disciples at Jesus' tomb.

You could also add to your prayer space Bible verses suitable for different days. (There are some suggestions at the back of the book, or on our web site, www.livelent.net)

Creating time for prayer

Think about creating time in the day for praying together as a family. You might want to make a promise to each other that you will try to do this every day during Lent. Family members might prefer to spend time alone in the prayer space. Make sure this is respected.

Here is another way of praying together:

Practise the examen

The 'examen' is a Christian practice that involves reflecting on the day and thinking about when you felt close to God and when you felt far from God. The idea is to identify patterns and to make changes, so that you can spend more time feeling close to God and avoid those things that take you away from God.

The Foster family of Birmingham, including ten-year-old twins Harriet and Thomas and six-year-old Joel, do a simple version of this review every day as part of their family evening mealtime.

Mum Jessica says:

"We have chosen supper-time to do this, as it is the only time we are all together. We ask everyone which was the best bit and which was the worst bit of the day. Sometimes we ask, 'When did you feel close to God?' and, 'When did you feel distant from God?'"

"The youngest (now six) starts, and when he has chosen his bit of the day he 'nominates' who is to go next. It couldn't be simpler, but we have found it helpful as a family to review what brings us joy and what drags us down."

The Foster Family

Harriet

Harriet, aged ten, says:

"It is good to share about the day; it is good to thank God for the good bits, and you might be able to find ways of preventing the bad bits."

At the end of the examen, you might want to say a prayer together, like this one, or use the Lord's Prayer.

> Dear God,
> Thank you for today.
>
> We are grateful for the good things . . . (everyone could say one thing out loud).
>
> We bring before you the hard things . . . (add your own situations, if appropriate).
>
> Help us to see you more clearly,
> love you more dearly,
> and follow you more nearly,
> day by day.
>
> Amen.

Creating Sabbath time as a family

The Jewish Sabbath was a day of rest in the week. It reflects the fact that God rested on the seventh day of creation. Lent is like a Sabbath in the Christian year — it is a time to cut back and slow down, and to enjoy rest. The hectic pace of life today, the many demands on our lives and the many new forms of entertainment on offer (TV/DVDs, computers, games consoles, etc.) can make it difficult to enjoy Sabbath time together. **Love Life Live Lent** encourages us to take time out to enjoy a slower pace of life, through stillness, connecting with nature, or doing something we really enjoy.

Here are some suggestions

1 Have a 'spend nothing' day: try to go a whole day without buying anything.

2 Have a 'no screens' day or evening: switch off the TV, computer, games console and mobiles — play games together instead. Why not invite someone from outside the family circle to join you?

3 Do a creative activity together, such as gardening, messing around with paints, clay or collage — do something even the youngest can join in with! Make the aim to have fun playing with the materials and to enjoy the experience, rather than to produce perfect works of art.

4 Gather together some objects that are fun to touch, feel and smell — such as a piece of velvet, feathers, a tray of sand, lavender bags, or pine cones. Spend some time enjoying the different textures and scents.

5 Make some simple vegetable soup together. Everyone can join in and help by chopping vegetables, stirring, or setting the table.

There are several recipes on the Internet, including one at www.utterlyrecipes.com/?p=17

LIFE FACT

Children in the UK spend an average of five hours a day in front of a TV or computer screen

Week 4 Kids' Actions

 **Action 19** Turn off the tap when brushing your teeth ☐

 **Action 22**

 **Action 20** Hold doors open for others ☐

Offer to help your ☐ teacher with a task

 **Action 21**

Give a home-made gift to a loved one ☐

 **Action 23**

Help stop global climate change: recycle your rubbish ☐

 **Action 24** Go for a walk in your neighbourhood (with an adult) and pray about what you see ☐

Adult & Youth Actions

Action 19
Have coffee or lunch with someone you don't know very well □

Action 22
Turn off the tap when brushing your teeth □

Buy something from a charity shop and reverse haggle □

Action 20

Action 23

Defrost your fridge and find out how climate change affects poor countries* □

Give a home -made gift to a loved one □

Action 21

Action 24

Go for a walk in your neighbourhood and pray about what you see □

Mothering Sunday / Refreshment Sunday

Lent facts

Mothering Sunday is the fourth Sunday of Lent. It is also known as Refreshment Sunday, because traditionally it was a day when the Lenten fast could be broken.

It is often called 'Mother's Day' and is a day when mothers are thanked, celebrated and given flowers and gifts. 'Mother's Day' is a recent invention, but 'Mothering Sunday' has ancient roots.

Some people think that 'Mothering Sunday' derives its name from Victorian times, when girls in domestic service would be given a day off to visit their mothers, taking flowers home with them.

There is an older tradition that 'Mothering Sunday' was the day during Lent when churchgoers would visit their home or 'mother' church.

While it is good to celebrate mothers on this day, we also need to be sensitive to those who do not have mothers – who have been separated from them through death, or for other reasons. It might be good to thank on this day those who have been like mothers – such as carers, teachers and teaching assistants – and to make sure they are given gifts too.

Why not:

- Take a large box or tin of chocolates to church for everyone to share

- Make a 'thank you' card for someone who has cared for you and post it to them anonymously.

Things to make for Mothering Sunday

Simnel cake is associated with both Mothering Sunday and Easter Sunday. You can find a recipe at www.bbc.co.uk/food/recipes/database/simnelcake_792.shtml, among other sites.

Here are some easy-to-make gift ideas:

- Put some seeds in an envelope (e.g. nasturtiums, which are fast-growing); decorate the outside of the envelope.

- Put some seeds in a plant pot and decorate the plant pot, e.g. with a ribbon and some paints.

- Decorate a glass jar — e.g. an empty jam jar — and put flowers in it.

- Make a photo-frame out of cardboard. You will need one piece for the back and one for the front. Cut a shape for photograph in the front sheet. There are endless possibilities for decorating your frame:
  - o Dried pasta shapes
  - o Lolly sticks
  - o Glitter
  - o Cut-out shapes

- Make a bookmark out of a piece of card. Stick a piece of ribbon or string onto the bottom to make the 'marker'. Younger children can dip fingers in paint to decorate, or use felt-tip pens, glitter, etc.

- Cut a heart shape out of card. Decorate it with smaller hearts cut out of crepe or tissue paper, or with sequins and glitter. Make a hole in the top and thread through a piece of wool, string or ribbon, so that it may be hung. Write a message on the back — or younger children may want to add a handprint in paint.

Grandparents around the world

Grandparents, if they are still around, are important figures! For some children in the UK and around the world, grandparents rather than parents are the main carers. In some countries affected by HIV/AIDS, grandparents are often having to care for grandchildren who have lost their parents to the disease.

Charities working in developing countries aim to support all those in need, including parents and grandparents. There are some particular projects aimed at supporting grandparents, such as Help the Aged's 'sponsor a grandparent' around the world project (www.sponsoragrandparent.org.uk), and The Mothers' Union has a project that enables you to send a gift (such as a goat!) to improve the lives of mothers and carers in the developing world – see www.makeamothersday.org

These stories are from Christian Aid:

Christian Aid / Amanda Farrant

Crafty grandmas

Grandmas are often great at thinking up craft activities for a rainy day. But in Kyrgyzstan some creative older women are setting up businesses based on their felt-making skills. This means that they can add to their income and afford to buy essentials like food and fuel to heat their homes. It also means that those who do not have family nearby have friends to talk to.

Why not have a go at making felt? See www.feltbetter.com/feltMaking.asp

If this seems too ambitious, why not make some Mother's Day or Easter gifts out of felt? (Felt can be glued, so you won't need a needle and thread.) You could try:

- A bookmark: cut shapes out of felt to stick on: e.g. flowers, Easter eggs
  - A pencil container: wrap some felt around a metal can.
    - Hair slides and brooches: buy some plain hair slides or metal badges, wrap them in felt and decorate.

A helping hand

In countries where many of the population have died because of illnesses related to HIV, children often go to live with their grandmas. Although it's great that children who have lost their parents can stay with other members of their family, sometimes the new responsibilities are difficult to cope with. In South Africa, projects like the Thandanani Children's Foundation (www.thandanani.org.za) help families where the grandma looks after everyone. They help with food parcels, school uniforms and other essentials the family could not afford otherwise.

Pray for grandparents who have to take on the responsibilities of caring for grandchildren in their old age. Also pray for HIV/AIDS orphans around the world, who have lost parents to the disease. You might like to use this prayer:

> ## Dear God,
> ### We pray for all those affected by disease around the world.
> ### We pray for grandparents who take in orphaned children.
> ### We pray for children who have lost parents.
> ### We ask that they would know your comfort and strength.
> ### Amen.

Mothers to the community

Proving that you're never too old to learn new skills — midwives in Haiti are learning more about hygiene. That means that the women they look after have a much better chance of having healthy babies and staying healthy themselves. The simple care that midwives provide at an important time means that they could be thought of as mothers to the community.

St John Ambulance

Young First Aiders

Older children might like to find out about learning some simple first aid. St John Ambulance runs Young First Aider courses for 7- to 16-year-olds. Find out more at www.sja.org.uk — click on the links for young people or call 08700 1049500.

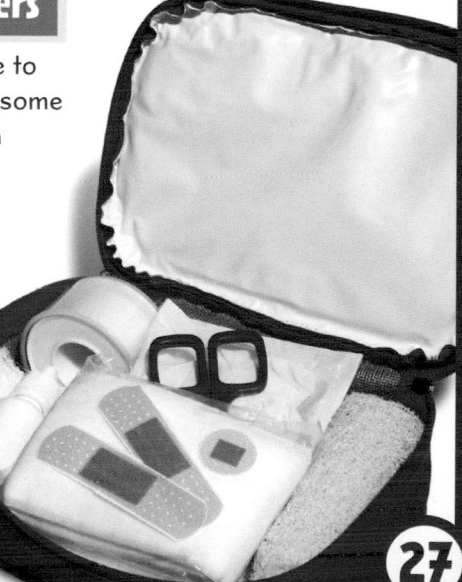

Week 5 Kids' Actions

 **Action 25**
Show an adult or carer how to do something they can't do ☐

 **Action 28**
Lend a friend a good book/CD/DVD or game ☐

 **Action 26**
Plant some seeds where the flowers will be seen ☐

 **Action 29**
Find out about children in a developing country you haven't heard of* ☐

 **Action 27**
Have a conversation with someone older than you ☐

 **Action 30**
Say a prayer for someone who is unwell or in need ☐

Adult & Youth Actions

Offer to babysit for friends ☐

Action 25

Action 28

Plant some seeds where the flowers will be seen ☐

Give blood ☐

Action 26

Action 27

Read the international section of a newspaper or web site for a week* ☐

Action 29

Buy something that is in season from a local shop ☐

Action 30

Say a prayer for someone who is ☐ unwell or in need

Preparing for new life

In the northern hemisphere, Lent takes place during late winter/early spring. The earth is waking up from a time when it has seemed asleep. But underneath the hard earth and winter snows, things have been growing, ready to shoot forth in the spring.

Planting seeds

Now is a good time to plant some seeds. One of the **Love Life Live Lent** actions for week 5 is to plant some seeds where the flowers will be seen.

What you will need

- Small plant pots
- Soil
- Seeds – you can buy these from garden centres. Suitable things to plant include grass seeds, sunflower seeds, lettuce, herbs, nasturtium seeds, etc.
- Labels – either 'lolly stick' labels or labels to stick on the pots. Write the names of the seeds you have planted on the labels.

Another activity

Let a few grass seeds grow in a small pot. When the grass is a few centimetres high, dig into the pot again and see what has happened to the seed. Only an empty shell is left, but all that new life has come out of it.

Jesus often told stories about seeds. You might like to look these up yourself:
- The story of the mustard seed (Matthew 13.31-2);
- The story of the sower (Matthew 13.3-9, 18-23).

Seed quiz

Which seeds grow into which plants?
(Answers on p. 48)

1

A

2

B

3

C

4

D

Viewing a sunset and sunrise

Over the weekend, why not go for a walk and catch the sun setting in the late afternoon? The next day, get up early and see if you can catch the sun rising.
(TIP: If you check your local weather forecast on the BBC weather site, it will give you the times for sunset and sunrise: www.bbc.co.uk/weather/ukweather/index.shtml)

Feeding the birds

During the winter and spring, birds may appreciate extra food being put out for them — food is scarcer at this time and in the spring birds may begin to rear families. Birds enjoy the following:

- Sunflower seeds (black ones are better)
- Peanuts (not dry-roasted or salted, though)
- Bird cakes.

You can make a simple bird cake by pouring some melted fat (suet or lard, not polyunsaturated fats such as margarine) over a mixture of nuts, seeds, dried fruit, oatmeal and cheese. You should use one-third fat to two-thirds dry mixture. Pour the mixture into a container to harden. There is a step-by-step recipe on the RSPB's youth site: www.rspb.org.uk/youth/makeanddo/activities/birdcake.asp

Going for a nature walk

If you have a park or countryside near you, go for a 'nature walk' and see how many different kinds of plants, birds and animals you can spot. Look for signs of spring and new life, such as:

- Bees buzzing round opening flowers
- Opening buds
- Early butterflies
- Birds building nests.

Being greener as a family

Lent can be a time to cut back on what we consume. Fasting from food makes us think of those who do not have enough to eat. Cutting back on buying things makes us aware of those who do not have enough in the rest of the world. It also reminds us of our responsibility to use what we have wisely, and to think about the impact of the way we live on our neighbours, both local and global.

There is plenty of advice now available to help us cut back on energy consumption. Most of it concerns Reducing, Recycling and Reusing.

Reduce

- Everyone in the family can think of ways to cut back on using water — e.g. turning off the tap when brushing your teeth; reusing washing-up water for watering plants.
- Everyone can switch off TVs, computers and mobile-phone chargers when they have finished with them, rather than leaving them on standby, and switch off lights when they leave the room.
- If you have a garden or outside space, why not have a go at growing your own vegetables, rather than being reliant on supermarkets. If space is limited, why not try growing some herbs?
  - Can you walk a journey, or take public transport, rather than driving?

Recycle

- Children can have fun helping to sort rubbish for recycling.
- Take your unwanted goods to a charity shop, advertise them on www.freerecycle.org or www.freecycle.org, or give them to a local project.
- Some organizations, including some charities, will take old mobile phones, printer cartridges, etc — go to (for example) Greensource Solutions (www.greensource.co.uk) and follow the link for recycling.

Reuse

- Make sure you use both sides of any paper you use.
- Scrap paper can be made up into notebooks, which can be given away as gifts.
- Reuse your plastic water bottles.
- If possible, mend things when they go wrong, instead of just replacing them.

What's your best reduce/recycle/reuse tip? Let us know at share@livelent.net!

Week 6 Kids' Actions

 **Action 31** Find out about life as a refugee and spend the night in a tent* ☐

 **Action 32**

Help a ☐ parent or carer with the shopping

Action 34

Feed the birds ☐

Action 35

Pick up some litter ☐

Action 33 Give a lollipop to your lollipop person ☐

 **Action 36** Make a palm cross and give it away* ☐

Adult & Youth Actions

Action 31 Email or write to your MP about a global poverty issue ☐

Action 34

Feed the birds ☐

Action 32 Contact a family member you haven't seen for a while ☐

Action 35

Pick up some litter ☐

Action 33

Give someone an apple ☐

Action 36 Make a palm cross and give it away* ☐

Passiontide and Palm Sunday

Lent Facts: Passiontide

'Passiontide' begins on the fifth Sunday of Lent. The word 'Passion' comes from the Latin for suffering, and it is a time when we begin to think about Jesus' suffering in the days before his crucifixion. The sixth Sunday of Lent is known as Palm Sunday and marks the start of Holy Week, during which Christians remember the last days of Jesus' earthly life.

During this week of **Love Life Live Lent**, as we prepare for Palm Sunday and the beginning of Holy Week, it is good to focus on the sufferings of others around the world — and to think about how we might help.

Lent Facts: Palm Sunday

Palm Sunday marks Jesus' triumphal entry into Jerusalem. Jesus, riding on a donkey, was cheered by the crowds, who waved palm branches and placed them in his path, crying 'Hosanna to the Son of David!' ('Hosanna' is a cry of praise, meaning 'Please save' in Hebrew). But only a few days later, the same crowds would call for Jesus to be crucified.

 You can read the story yourself in Matthew chapter 21, verses 1-16.

 Watch the scene from **The Miracle Maker**, end of scene 11, from 49:06 to 51:42.

Some churches have special processions on Palm Sunday — there might even be a donkey!

Decorate your home with palm branches

What you will need

Large sheets of card or stiff paper
Scissors
Blu-tack™
Paints and crayons, etc

Method

You could make two small palms, cut out of paper or card, and place these around a doorframe. They could also be added to your 'sacred space', or placed around your Lenten tree.

If you want to take it further, you can make an arch of palms to place over your front door for Palm Sunday. Cut two palm-branch shapes (see diagram) big enough to reach from the bottom to the top of your front door. Score down the centre of each branch and fold back gently, until the palm has a slight curve. Add decoration to the branch if you wish.

You could also decorate your door using greenery from the garden.

Making a Palm cross

There are some simple instructions at http://www.kidssundayschool.com/index.php - search under 'Palm leaf cross'.

Helping those who are suffering

Small is beautiful

Love Life Live Lent is all about being kind and generous to others. Sometimes we can feel helpless in the face of so much suffering around the world. But small things can make a big impact. Here are some examples from Christian Aid, a charity working round the world to help people in need.

Did you know that a handful of worms can help farmers in the Philippines increase their crop of rice? The worms multiply, and the extras are passed on to other farmers. Over time, the handful of worms becomes two handfuls and can help even more people.

What sort of difference do you think a simple broom can make? They keep houses tidy, but in Egypt an organization called Coptic Orthodox Churches Bless uses brooms for more than cleaning. Bless provide a small loan to a family to buy the materials to make brooms. The family can then sell these brooms to pay for essentials such as food and shelter. In time, the families can make enough money to pay back the loan.

Did you know guinea pigs can help fight tuberculosis (TB)? In Peru, Alberto was recovering from TB and couldn't work. He started breeding guinea pigs to sell. These helped him to buy enough food to eat well — which is really important for people recovering from serious illnesses such as TB.

What can you do?

You can be a blessing to people around the world by taking small actions, such as:

- Praying for change. Here is a prayer (with actions!) to use with your family:

> ## Dear God
>
> **Although we are quite small**
> **(crouch down into a ball)**
>
> **And the world seems very big**
> **(stand up and raise arms high above heads)**
>
> **Please help us to see (put hands to eyes**
> **as if looking through binoculars)**
>
> **That we can be strong**
> **(put arms up to show muscles)**
>
> **And help make wrong things right**
> **(shake finger from side to side for 'wrong'**
> **and then do thumbs-up for 'right')**
>
> ## Amen

- Helping to buy some worms/brooms/guinea pigs by donating money saved during Lent, or fundraising, for charities such as Christian Aid.

- Speaking out on behalf of poor people — one of this week's suggested actions for adults and young people is to write a letter to your MP to ask what they will do to help developing countries.

- Getting in the know — find out more about people's lives in other countries and tell others about it. See, for example, www.christianaid.org.uk (children's site: www.globalgang.org); www.tearfund.org (children's site: http://actionpack.tcarfund.org); www.worldvision.org.uk

- A number of charities now run schemes that enable you to buy a really useful gift for communities in the developing world — such as some worms, goats, or clean water. See www.presentaid.org (Christian Aid) or www.livinggifts.org.uk (Tearfund), among others.

Week 7 Holy Week Kids' Actions

Action 37

Give someone a ☐
Fairtrade Easter egg

Watch a film ☐
about Jesus' life

Action 38

Action 39

Make hot
cross buns and
share them ☐

Action 40

Polish someone's
shoes for them ☐

Make or draw an
Easter garden in
a place that will
be seen ☐

Action 41

Celebrate Easter.
Alleluia! ☐

Action 42

Adult & Youth Actions

 **Action 37** Watch a film ☐ about Jesus' life

 **Action 38**

Buy a Fairtrade Easter egg ☐

Polish someone's shoes for them ☐

 **Action 39**

 **Action 40**

Make hot cross buns and share them ☐

 **Action 41** Make or draw an Easter garden in a place that will be seen by passers-by ☐

 **Action 42** Celebrate Easter. Alleluia! ☐

Holy Week

Lent Facts: Holy Week

Holy Week begins with Palm Sunday and concludes with Holy Saturday (also known as Easter Eve – the day before Easter Sunday). It marks the events of the last week of Jesus' life.

Lent Facts: Maundy Thursday

Maundy Thursday marks Jesus' 'Last Supper' with his disciples. 'Maundy' comes from 'mandatum', which is Latin for 'command', because at this meal Jesus washed the disciples' feet and told them that they should love one another. (Can you guess which of the **Love Life Live Lent** actions is for Maundy Thursday?) As they celebrated the meal together, Jesus gave thanks, broke the unleavened bread and shared it with his disciples. He then took the cup of wine, blessed it and shared it. Christians do the same in Holy Communion/Eucharist services today, to remember what Jesus did.

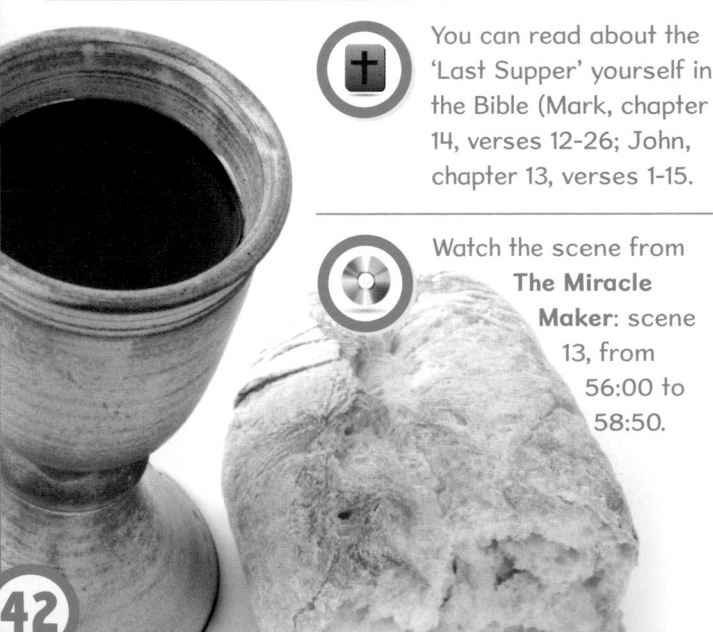

 You can read about the 'Last Supper' yourself in the Bible (Mark, chapter 14, verses 12-26; John, chapter 13, verses 1-15.

Watch the scene from **The Miracle Maker**: scene 13, from 56:00 to 58:50.

Lent Facts: The Passover meal

The 'last supper' Jesus ate with his disciples was a Passover meal. Jewish people eat this meal to remember how God delivered their ancestors from slavery in Egypt. (God 'passed over' their homes, which were marked with the blood of a lamb, but struck down the firstborn of the Egyptians.)

 You can read the story yourself in the Old Testament part of the Bible, in the book of Exodus, chapter 12.

 Watch the scene in the DVD **The Prince of Egypt**.

Lent Facts: Good Friday

Good Friday marks the event of Jesus' death on the cross. It is called 'good' because Christians believe that Jesus showed God's love by dying on the cross. Some churches hold a three-hour service between 12 noon and 3.00 pm on Good Friday.

 You can read about the events yourself in John, chapters 18 and 19, or in any of the other Gospels (Matthew, Mark and Luke).

Watch the scene from **The Miracle Maker**. For the whole story, watch scenes 16 and 17 (from 1:06:00 to 1:13:30).

In England, the Queen gives away 'Maundy money' every year at a special Maundy Thursday service. How much money does she give away? And to how many people?
(Answer on p. 48).

Passover meal

Have a Passover or Seder meal. You can find instructions at www.wf-f.org/Seder.html

Each part of the meal means something special. A typical Passover meal includes:

- **Roast lamb** – to remember the lambs that were killed, and their blood sprinkled on the doorposts of the Jewish people.

- **An egg** – various meanings have been suggested. As eggs get harder as they are boiled, some think this represents the fact that the Jewish people held on to their beliefs under slavery in Egypt. Others say it represents the new life of freedom.

- **Parsley** (or horseradish or romaine lettuce) – representing 'bitter herbs', symbolizing the bitterness of living as slaves. The parsley may be dipped in salt water to represent tears.

- **Unleavened bread** (e.g. Matzos) – unleavened bread has no yeast in it and is therefore flat: it represents the bread the Jews made in a hurry when they left Egypt – they had no time to let the yeast rise.

- **Charoseth** – a mixture of chopped-up apples, nuts, honey, sugar, cinnamon and red wine. This is like the cement that held together the bricks the Israelites made in captivity.

- **Red wine** – at a Jewish Passover meal, four cups of wine are drunk, to represent the four times God promised freedom to the Jewish people in Egypt. Wine is also a symbol of freedom and joy.

Cross activities

- Make 14 crosses out of card and number them 1 to 14. On Passion Sunday (the fifth Sunday of Lent), hang the cross numbered 14 on your Lenten tree. Hang up one cross each day until you reach Easter.

- Make a Passion cross: draw a cross shape on card and divide it into six spaces (see diagram). On Good Friday, decorate five of the spaces with scenes from the last week of Jesus' life.

For example:
- Palm Sunday (Matthew 21.1-9 or John 12.12-16)
- The Last Supper (Mark 14.22-24)
- Jesus' arrest in the Garden (Luke 22.47-54)
- Jesus condemned to death (Matthew 27.20-26)
- The crucifixion (Luke 23.26-46)

Leave the central space blank for a picture of the stone rolled away from the tomb – add this on Easter Sunday.

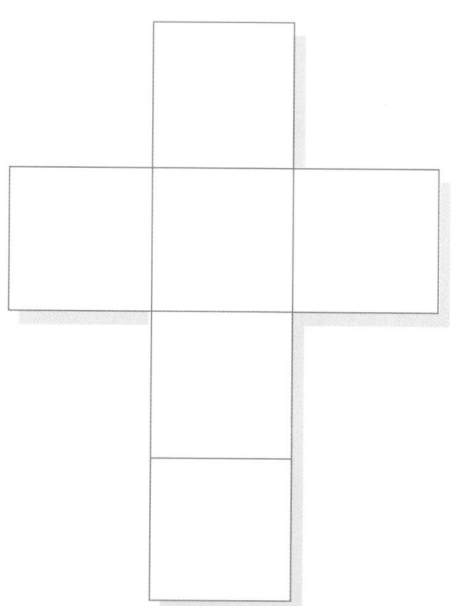

Hot cross buns

These are eaten on Good Friday, as the cross shape is a reminder of the cross on which Jesus died. Buns were traditionally eaten by Romans and Greeks to honour their gods. Christians do the same to remember Jesus. One of the **Love Life Live Lent** actions this week suggests making some and sharing them.

Ingredients

(makes about 22 buns)
150 g (6 oz) strong white flour
150 g (6 oz) strong wholemeal flour
1 teaspoon salt
1 teaspoon mixed spice
50 g (2 oz) soft light brown sugar
50 g (2 oz) butter
150 g (5 oz) currants
50 g (2 oz) candied mixed peel
1 sachet easy-blend yeast
300 ml (½ pt) milk, warmed
2 medium eggs, beaten

For the crosses:
125 g (4 ½ oz) plain white flour
45 ml (2 fl oz) vegetable oil
90 ml (3 fl oz) cold water

For the glaze:
2 tablespoons honey or golden syrup, warmed

Note: as before, use either metric or imperial measurements; don't mix them.

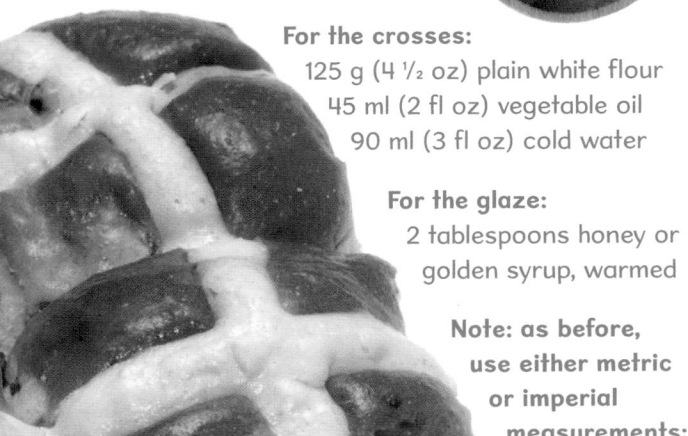

What to do

1. Preheat the oven to 200°C (400°F, gas mark 6).
2. Place the flour, salt, spice and sugar in a bowl. Rub in the butter, then add the currants and peel. Then stir in the yeast.
3. Warm the milk until you are still just able to put your finger into it, then add it to the flour mixture along with the eggs. Mix well to form a dough.
4. Turn onto a floured surface and knead lightly until smooth and elastic — this should take about ten minutes.
5. Place the dough in a clean bowl, cover and leave to rise in a warm place for an hour, until doubled in size.
6. Turn out onto a floured surface and knead again for two minutes.
7. Divide the dough into 22 pieces and form into balls. Place on an oiled baking sheet and mark a cross on the top of each bun with a sharp knife. Cover and leave in a warm place for 20–30 minutes, until doubled in size again.
8. Mix together the flour and oil and mix in the cold water. Using a piping bag, pipe a cross onto each bun.
9. Cook for 15 minutes, or until brown.
10. When the buns are cooked, brush them with warm honey or golden syrup and leave to cool on a wire rack.

If you want to try an unusual alternative, try making 'Resurrection rolls'. See recipe at http://www.dltk-kids.com/recipes/resurrection_rolls.htm

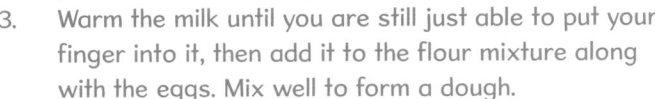

Making an Easter garden

This would be a good day to make or draw an Easter garden and place it where it might be seen by others. You can collect some of the natural materials from your garden, or go for a walk and see if you can find them.

You will need

You will need:

- A few good-sized stones
- Some moss
- Twigs to make three crosses
- String or thread to bind the twigs together
- Some soil or sand
- A tray or baking tray
- Some tinfoil
- An eggcup or small vase.

What to do

1. Line the tray with foil and fill it with sand or soil.

2. Use the stones to build the tomb. Choose a nice round stone to make the door.

3. Make a space in the soil for an eggcup and fill it with water and flowers; or you could plant primulas or other small plants in the soil to look like grass.

4. Make the crosses, using the twigs and string or thread, and stick them in the soil.

Remember to move the stone from the tomb on Easter Day!

If you don't want to make a garden using soil and greenery, you can make one out of a shoebox.

1. Colour the inside of the box with green paint or felt pen.
2. Decorate it with cut-out paper flowers.
3. Make three crosses out of lolly sticks. Stick them upright at one end, using sticky tape.

Or use a plastic yoghourt pot – you will need one of the square ones that has a separate corner compartment. Clean out the pot. Bend up the corner compartment. (This will form the cave.) Draw a stone on a piece of paper and stick this over the mouth of the cave. Add Easter greenery to the rest of the pot. On Easter Sunday, remove the stone from over the cave and replace with paper, on which you have written 'He is risen!'

You can use the garden to talk about Good Friday and then, on Saturday night, roll back the stone and sprinkle chocolate eggs in the garden, to be found on Sunday morning.

Lent facts: Holy Saturday

This marks the day when Jesus lay in the tomb. It is a day to reflect on Jesus' death and to prepare for the marking of his resurrection on Easter Sunday. Some people try to make this a quieter day than usual, to help them remember Jesus.

Easter Sunday

This marks Jesus' resurrection from the dead. It is a day of celebration and joy.

 Read the story yourself in John, chapter 20, verses 1-18.

 Watch the story in **The Miracle Maker**, scenes 18 and 19, from 1:14:45 to the end.

Activities for Easter Sunday

- Have an Easter-egg hunt. Eggs are a symbol of new life.
- Share some simnel cake or chocolate crispies decorated with small chocolate eggs and chicks.

Some Easter greetings

The following 'greetings' are traditionally used on Easter Sunday. You might like to use one of them on Easter Sunday morning, after you have rolled away the stone in your Easter garden. Make sure you shout the 'Alleluias'! Parts everyone joins in are printed in bold.

> One person says:
> Alleluia. Christ is risen.
>
> Everyone replies:
> **He is risen indeed. Alleluia.**

> Or use this extended version:
>
> Jesus Christ is risen from the dead.
> **Alleluia.**
>
> He has defeated the powers of death.
> **Alleluia.**
>
> Jesus turns our sorrow into dancing.
> **Alleluia.**
>
> He has the words of eternal life.
> **Alleluia.**

Keeping going after Lent and Easter

Love Life Live Lent ends at Easter but the activities don't have to stop there. Here are some ways of keeping it going.

- Have a 'road to Emmaus' walk and talk. The risen Jesus met two disciples on the road to Emmaus (although they did not recognize him at first) and helped them to understand what had happened.

 You can read this story in the Bible, in Luke, chapter 24, verses 13-35,

 Watch it in **The Miracle Maker**, scene 19.

On your walk, ask everyone: what was most important to you about Lent and Easter?

Which **Love Life Live Lent** action made the greatest impact?

What would you like to continue doing as a family, now that Lent is over?

- You can keep your 'sacred space' going after Easter Sunday. You might like to add a flower each day until Pentecost (50 days after Easter Sunday).

Resources

Quiz answers

Shrove Tuesday quiz (p. 6)

1 - B
2 - A
3 - C

Seed quiz (p. 30)

1 - B
2 - A
3 - D
4 - C

Maundy Thursday question (p. 42)

The Queen distributes Maundy money in pence matching the years of her age to the same number of both men and women as her age. So in 2008 the Queen gave 82 pence in specially minted Maundy coins to 82 men and 82 women.

Charities working with children in the developing world

Christian Aid – www.christianaid.org.uk
Save the Children – www.savethechildren.org.uk
Tearfund – www.tearfund.org
World Vision – www.worldvision.org.uk

. . . and many others.

Bible versions and books

Bible references have been given for key events. You may prefer to read the stories in a children's Bible. Versions for under-7s are usually Bible stories, retold for younger children. Check that any version you choose is appropriate for the age of your child. **The Big Bible Storybook** (Scripture Union, 2006) is popular for younger children.

Other books

Charlotte Ryton, **The Lion Book of 5-Minute Parables**, Lion, 2008, includes the story of the sower (see p. 30)

Two board books for younger children featuring the events of Palm Sunday:
Kathleen Long Bostrom, **Easter, Easter, Almost here!** Zondervan, 2005
Alice Joyce Davidson, **My Day with Jesus**, Zondervan, 2005

The following books include the events of the Easter story:
Jan Godfrey, **The Road to Easter**, Bible Reading Fellowship, 2008
Christina Goodings, **I want to know about Jesus**, Lion, 2008
Bob Hartman, **Easter Stories**, Lion, 2005
Lois Rock, **A Child's First Story of Jesus**, Lion, 2004
Lois Rock, Easter: **The Ever-lasting story**, Lion, 2004
Andrea Skevington, **The Story of Jesus**, Lion, 2007

Films

The Miracle Maker (U, Icon Films) animated version of the life of Jesus

The Prince of Egypt (U, Dreamworks) animated version of the Exodus story

Storykeepers (2 DVDs) the last four episodes focus on Lent and Easter. See www.storykeepers.com